VISION OF HOPE

VISION OF HOPE

Compiled by
Benjamin Greene, Jr.

Judson Press®Valley Forge

VISION OF HOPE

Copyright © 1988
Judson Press, Valley Forge, PA 19482–0851

Unless otherwise indicated, all Scripture quotations are from the Revised Standard Version of the Bible copyrighted 1946, 1952 © 1971, 1973 by the Division of Christian Education of the National Council of the Churches of Christ in the U.S.A., and used by permission.

Other Scripture quotations are taken from the *Good News Bible,* the Bible in Today's English Version, Copyright © American Bible Society, 1976. Used by permission. HOLY BIBLE New International Version, copyright © 1978, New York International Bible Society. Used by permission.

Library of Congress Cataloging-in-Publication Data

Vision of hope/compiled by Ben Greene, Jr.
   p.   cm.
  ISBN 0-8170-1150-1
  1. American Baptist Churches in the U.S.A.—Sermons. 2. Community development—Religious aspects—Baptists—Sermons. 3. Baptists —Sermons. 4. Sermons, American. 5. Church and the world—Sermons.
I. Greene, Ben.
BX6333.A1V57   1988
252'.06131—dc19   88-28256
                                                               CIP

The name JUDSON PRESS is registered as a trademark in the U.S. Patent Office.

Contents

Preface

American Baptist Churches affirm the biblical hope of a renewed world made possible by God's redemptive activity through Jesus Christ. The historic mission of American Baptist Churches has been establishing churches and building communities. Through Church-Based Community Development, American Baptists are responding to discouraged persons and communities with a Vision of Hope.

Many communities in our nation are in despair, evidenced by the fragmentation and suffering which are not consistent with the wholeness and hope of the biblical faith. These anxieties of survival are mirrored in many of our congregations. As the late Jitsuo Morikawa said:

> Many churches, families, institutions, communities, even our personal lives, suffer from existence as a frozen people. We have plenty of assets, magnitudes of talent, expertise of knowledge, but we seem unable to command it, to have it at our disposal in the right form when we need it.

National data on income, unemployment, underemployment, poverty, housing, and employment of women show the extent of distress in our communities. These statistics call our denomination to make the quest for new life a priority.

Confronted with the despair and deep depression which dehumanizes persons, the Board of National Ministries, in collaboration with American Baptist Regions, has determined to move in a concerted effort to renew communities through

American Baptist congregations located in these communities.

The gospel is interpreted as participation in the realm of God, made known in Jesus. From that foundation National Ministries intends to create Visions of Hope through Church-Based Community Development.

Church-Based Community Development is a program designed to enable American Baptist congregations to provide resources, consultation, and practical "hands-on" skills for involvement in a community ministry which relates to the structures, to the issues of the people, and which empowers people living within the community.

Church-Based Community Development offers an effective and unique strategy for dealing with the problems of persons in poverty and the powerless in underdeveloped communities. As an intervention strategy, Church-Based Community Development does not seek to make the existing conditions in a community more bearable. This program seeks to change the structures of the community by building permanent institutions which empower citizens of the community to play a more active role in the control of the community's resources.

An example of this approach may be found in the First Baptist Church of Los Angeles. Motivated by a sense of mission, First Baptist has mobilized its spiritual and human resources to respond to issues of human need in its community. This church has developed programs that link families in the area with existing public and private services designed to enhance and maintain life, health and dignity. The church has also expressed active concern about the availability and use of illegal drugs in the community. The church is determined to help at-risk youth and predelinquent juveniles develop the self-esteem, courage and values required to say no! to drug use.

The reality of issues of injustice and the need for societal change continue to characterize our times. Growing immigrant populations, widening economic disparity, rapid technological change and the destruction of the environment adversely affect the opportunities of minorities in our society to achieve economic well-being and personal and social fulfillment.

Church-Based Community Development will provide the following opportunities to impact these situations:

1) American Baptists' racial and ethnic diversity can help to raise the denomination's consciousness about justice issues as they are experienced by minorities among us. As "wounded healers" these minority persons need our support in their pain and struggle as well as our encouragement to be our teachers in responding to justice issues, particularly at the community level.

2) Local American Baptist congregations will be enabled to see and respond to justice issues that affect not only the general masses in our society but also impact particular groups in our own denominational family as well as people struggling for self-esteem, self-reliance and self-fulfillment in the neighborhoods of our churches.

3) American Baptist Churches' resources will be linked with those of other organizations who have similar goals and objectives for mutual support, thereby enabling American Baptist agencies, entities and congregations to respond effectively to community justice issues.

One of the basic questions involved in Church-Based Community Development is: Are congregations willing to get involved in the struggle to transform their communities and thereby impact the world? Even healthy congregations will not remain healthy in dying communities. The vitality and relevance of the church is connected to the health of the community. The gospel challenges us to see life in all of its interrelated components. Local congregations know that people cannot fend for themselves when they are denied their basic dignity and rights. Churches are called to participate in the empowering work of redemption leading to the affirmation of faith and life. Congregations can become affirming and sustaining bodies of faith and can celebrate God's mission in the world through Church-Based Community Development.

Dr. Benjamin Greene, Jr.
January, 1988

Introduction

by Benjamin Greene, Jr.

There are numerous scriptural references one could use to call a congregation to involvement in its community, giving a Vision of Hope to people in need. For a Vision of Hope to occur members of the congregation must first hear the call of God: a call for wholeness, salvation, justice, righteousness, transformation and hope. Jesus commissions disciples to be ministers of healing, helping and freeing so that people of God become agents of blessing to all the families of the earth.

It is our prayer that these sermons will serve as an inspiration to those of us who proclaim and practice God's Word, that the people may hear God's call. Some of these sermons were delivered at community development events, while others were written especially for this resource and two of the sermons were reprinted for this booklet.

It is our hope that the concerns, issues, and needs of people in the communities will be integrated in congregations' basic reason for existence. God's living presence is sensed in the ministries of a congregation in its community, and those ministering meet Jesus in the poor and ill. Community development in Jesus thus renews and strengthens the church.

I thank the authors of the sermons in this book for their spiritual and written contributions; and my wife, June Courtney, whose love, faith, deep spiritual life and interest in my efforts are a constant inspiration and encouragement to me.

The Reverend Doctor
Benjamin Greene, Jr.

The Reverend Benjamin Greene, Jr., is an American Baptist missionary, a member of the American Baptist Public Mission Team, and represents the American Baptist Black Caucus on the General Staff Council. He is the director of Community Development, Board of National Ministries, American Baptist Churches, USA, Valley Forge, Pennsylvania.

He is responsible for implementing and monitoring a Church-Based Community Development program. In collaboration with American Baptist Church Regions, it is his responsibility to provide resources and consultations to ABC entities on how to become involved in community/neighborhood ministry which relates to structure, community issues and concerns, and how to empower community residents.

Included in his duties are: working within the Church and Community Development Unit in the implementation of its goals; highlighting community development within the context of New Church Development and Church Renewal; broadening the denomination's vision for community ministry by providing consultations and training for National Ministries' staff, NCD pastors, Regional staff, et. al.

A Vision of Hope

by Benjamin Greene, Jr.

Where there is no vision the people perish (Proverbs 29:18, paraphrased)

Vision denote the revelation of God's will made through God's agents who direct the course of human events. The fatal effect of the absence of such revelation of God's will is confusion and disorder. People feel no reason to go on. They feel hopeless.

Many congregations and communities are tired and discouraged because they have no vision of the future to which they believe God is calling them. Individuals, as well as congregations, have no pictures of possibilities opened by God that compel them onward and give them a sense of purpose and hope.

God is calling the church to create a Vision of Hope. This vision is to be shared within the congregation and disseminated into the neighborhood, enabling people to take charge of their lives and create a community of faith. People need a vehicle of hope for their dreams, goals and ideas to become reality. People need a strong sense of "hope against hope" and a vision of new life that informs their day-to-day struggle.

In order to acquire a vision for the future of community and congregation, one must seek the will of God—God's plan,

God's expectations. One might pray, "not my will, O Lord, but let thy will be done."

I remember when I was taught the Lord's Prayer. It was during my early childhood when I had contracted diphtheria. I was aware that many children with this disease had died, and I thought the same thing would happen to me. But I could hear my sister, along with the neighborhood children, playing outside as I lay in bed longing to join them. All I wanted to do was get well and go outside and play. My mother and grandmother talked to me about the healing power of Jesus. They stressed the fact that all I needed was faith. Then, they encouraged me to pray. At that time in my life, all I knew was:

> Now I lay me down to sleep;
> I pray the Lord my soul to keep.
> If I should die before I wake,
> I pray the Lord my soul to take.

My mother and grandmother taught me Psalm 23 and the Lord's Prayer. I would lie there and repeat portions of both over and over again. Sometimes I would simply say, "Jesus, make me well." Gradually my health began to improve; my strength returned and I was able to get up, play with my sister and friends, and eventually return to school. I believed then, and I still believe, it was not just the doctor who brought me through, but the doctor under the guidance of God.

This is just one early childhood example of how God answered prayers in my life as I also meditated on Scripture during the time of prayer. I now know that there are numerous Scriptures that give meaning to each individual who has had an encounter with the Ground of his or her being. And there have been numerous occasions when prayers have been answered.

Jesus made prayer an important part of his teaching. Jesus prayed often. He prayed before every involvement of his ministry. He prayed at his baptism, the calling of the Twelve, the transfiguration, the raising of Lazarus, and on the cross. Jesus again and again told his followers if they wanted to live they should turn to God, who is the Source of life. He further instructed them that if they wished to be one body, they would need to learn ways which made for life in community.

The biblical record gives numerous occasions of persons seeking and finding the vision of God for their lives. Moses was forty days alone with the divine Presence on Horeb. Elijah fasted forty days in the wilderness before the vision and voice came to him. Ezekiel; Daniel; Isaiah; Peter; Paul; and John, the beloved apostle, were under the influence of the Holy Spirit. Their eyes were opened to see visions and sights. And their ears were unlocked to hear voices more clearly. Jesus was led by the Holy Spirit into the wilderness (Luke 4:1) for silence and solitude, for prayer and fasting, to determine what God's will was for him. God's word is always addressed to us as individuals and as a community as we seek to know and do our Creator's will.

Throughout the New Testament, Jesus showed by precept and example that God cares for every human being. No child was too small to escape his concern. Women, as well as troops of the occupying army—the Roman centurions—were not overlooked. Social outcasts, prostitutes and tax collectors heard the gospel. Poor people, who had neither status nor money, were the subjects of Jesus' special ministry. In short, Jesus included everyone in his ministry. This emphasis was expanded, under the driving influence of Paul, to include the Gentile world (Romans 1:16–18; 5:1–11).

To the multitudes Jesus offered hope and healing. Those who came to him with physical illnesses found help. He actually fed the crowds on at least two occasions. For Jesus, salvation was intended to restore persons to total wholeness. His death and resurrection atoned for sin and resulted in bringing isolated individuals into a new, Spirit-filled community.

Envisioning begins, then, with prayer and meditation on Scripture, seeking to learn the will of God. Other elements of the envisioning process include imagination, wishing, brainstorming, becoming aware of images from the arts and media, as well as Bible study and prayer. Each of these will be necessary as we seek God's vision for renewal of the communities which surround us.

The task of our American Baptist family as we seek to renew our communities will require the entire racial make-up of American Baptist churches. We must be willing to struggle first against the enemy within ourselves, including our individualism and our own political irresponsibility. We must also contend with our own victim mentality and our reluctance to live up to our fullest potential as partners with God in reconciling all things unto God.

We must accept rather than avoid the challenge and the necessity to transform less effective and discouraged American Baptist congregations in their quest for new life. For many of us this task is too awesome. We deliberately prefer to remain at the level of reaction or complaint or protest. We sense that if we once begin to think with more depth about the nature of our congregation, and how community and world issues such as racism, sexism, classism, and capitalism have been destroying our relationships with one another, ourselves, the world community and with God, we will also have to accept responsibility as American Baptists for decline of our congregations rather than blame the victims in our neighborhoods.

Consider this challenge from Benjamin Mays:

> It must be borne in mind, however, that the tragedy in life does not lie in not reaching your goal. The tragedy lies in having no goal to reach. It isn't a calamity to die with dreams unfulfilled, but it is a calamity not to dream. It is not a disaster to be unable to capture your ideal, but it is a disaster to have no ideal to capture. It is not a disgrace not to reach the stars, but it is a disgrace to have no stars to reach for. Not failure, but low aim is the sin.[1]

We must respond to God's vision by living our dreams, our ideals, by reaching for the unattainable goals as we aspire to bring new life to our churches and communities.

[1]Benjamin Mays, *What Man Lives By* (Valley Forge: Judson Press, 1972), p. 37.

The Reverend
Doctor William K. Cober

Dr. William K. Cober has been the executive director of National Ministries of the American Baptist Churches since 1977. In that position he works with an executive staff of 50 and over 150 missionaries in the United States and Puerto Rico. National Ministries seeks to encourage excellence in local churches, supports ministries on behalf of American Baptists and deals with the expression of faith on contemporary issues. He was a member of the Presidential Panel of the National Council of Churches which has created a new style of ecumenical ministry and a new organizational structure.

Prior to his current position, Cober was the executive minister of the Kansas Baptist Convention.

These last two positions were the result of broad experiences in local pastorates in Westfield, New Jersey; Dayton, Ohio; and Blackstone, Massachusetts.

His education was at Colgate University and the Andover Newton Theological School.

The Church of the Jericho Road

by William K. Cober

"A man was going down from Jerusalem to Jericho, and he fell among robbers, who stripped him and beat him, and departed, leaving him half dead. Now by chance a priest was going down that road; and when he saw him he passed by on the other side. So likewise a Levite, when he came to the place and saw him, passed by on the other side. But a Samaritan, as he journeyed, came to where he was; and when he saw him, he had compassion, and went to him and bound up his wounds, pouring on oil and wine; then he set him on his own beast and brought him to an inn, and took care of him. And the next day he took out two denarii and gave them to the innkeeper, saying, 'Take care of him; and whatever more you spend, I will repay you when I come back.' Which of these three, do you think, proved neighbor to the man who fell among the robbers?" He said, "The one who showed mercy on him." And Jesus said to him, "Go and do likewise." (Luke 10:30–37)

It's Sunday morning, a time for many to think about their options for the day. It could be a day of entertainment, of relaxing around the house, of doing a lot of errands that have piled up, or going to church. Many persons choose options other than church each week, but recently I've asked myself about those millions of people who are attending church most Sundays. How do they approach their church experience? Habit? Routine activity? Eagerness? Why do they choose to go to church?

A number of years ago I met a Puerto Rican botanist. He wanted to show me some of the thousands of varieties of orchids in the botanical gardens outside of Río Piedras. He took delight in each one and shared his dreams. The botanical gardens were to be without walls or gates, near to the crowds of the city and available as an oasis of beauty and quiet. With his knowledge of flowers he pictured every Puerto Rican home surrounded by beautiful flowers and saw raising flowers as a means of income for poor people.

He said he was about to retire but they would keep him on for $1 a year. He added wistfully, "I'll be the most overpaid person in Puerto Rico!" What makes someone choose to continue working when the motivation is not financial gain?

There are people who see life as routine, dull, something to last out. "Thank God It's Friday" is a common statement. There are also the zealots, the excited people, the people who feel they are making a difference and that the world is different because of their efforts. What makes the difference?

When Jesus tested the beliefs of those around him, he responded to Peter, "On the rock of your faith I will build my church and the powers of death shall not prevail against it." Can you imagine being singled out by the Master as a significant factor in the development of the Christian community and its witness? Jesus wasn't speaking of the church as buildings and organizations, but about the fact that those who took his message seriously could make a difference in this world. They would enable him to be known by others, be a means through which the will of God might be done. If you feel that God is counting deeply on you for some life-transforming and world-shaking activity, will that make a difference in your approach to living each day?

There is a familiar parable that suggests there is excitement and drama in the Christian adventure. The church can foster and encourage that mood. It comes from the fact that we are instruments by which God's purposes are clearly revealed. This parable of the good Samaritan tells of the traveller, the thieves, the people passing by the wounded man, the Samaritan, the innkeeper. The drama happened on the Jericho Road. Churches that understand and act on the drama of the good Samaritan might rename themselves "The Church of the Jericho Road."

What are the characteristics of the Church of the Jericho Road, and what do they say to us?

The Church of the Jericho Road Reacts

A man was travelling from Jerusalem to Jericho when he was attacked by robbers. They beat him and took what he had and left him lying by the road half dead. How does a Christian, how does a church respond to such a situation?

Church people walked by. Let's not condemn them too quickly. Two friends of mine have pulled over when signalled by a driver behind them. They both were attacked, brutally beaten and left wounded. One, when he became conscious, made his way to a farm house. If you had looked out and seen a big man, clothing torn and bleeding from serious wounds, in the middle of the night, in the isolation of a farm house, what would you do?

We have previously made a big thing about people going about their religious activities and not stopping to care for the wounded man by the side of the road. Jesus had scathing things to say about so-called religious people who ignored the needy or were hypocrites. But he told this story in answer to one question, "What is a person like who acts neighborly?" Obviously he had in mind someone who was willing to interrupt his/her own life and even share his/her own possessions to care for another.

The Church of the Jericho Road sees human need and reacts. It is sensitive to the issues of human existence, caring about the vulnerable and needy, willing to utilize its own resources to care for or meet a human need.

One church was located next to a Dairy Queen. In that small town the young people found that to be a convenient hangout. They not only lay on the lawn as they talked and fooled around, but they left a great deal of debris. The trustees of the church met to decide what to do with this situation. After surveying the many youth on their property, they decided to change the locks on the doors of the church, to make them stronger.

That was a church that chose not to react to apparent need or opportunity. It simply protected itself from the situation.

I remember years ago someone asking a Christian leader for advice. He said he rode the train to New York City from Connecticut. As he left the affluent suburbs, he found himself travelling on through poorer areas that were upsetting to him. But he could think of nothing to do about that. The Christian leader said that one thing he could do was to keep the shade up—be aware of the situation.

The church reacts. It brings peoples' needs into its services. It expresses concern about peace and justice in our world and lets its representatives in state and national congresses know that it cares. It surveys the community of which it is a part and asks questions. In one community the school superintendent said that over 50 percent of the children came from homes where they did not live with both of their parents. In another, it was apparent that children were on their own, "latch key children" at home alone after school until one of the parents came home.

The point is that the church reacts. It sees clearly the wounded and vulnerable, the lonely and distressed. It not only sees the needs within its own membership, but the needs of its community, its region, its state, its nation and the world. The problem with stained-glass windows is that sometimes they give us stained-glass hearts. The light of the real world is filtered into the church so that the real situation is not appreciated. Only beautiful colors are allowed. One time we saw a luxurious house located next to the town dump in a small community. That may not be where you or I would prefer to live, but it is appropriate for Christian people to see the human refuse, the temptations and tragedies that are part of our world, and to react—not with "we've got to get out of here" but "what does this information mean? How can we react to it in a loving way? How can we live in the midst and bring change?"

The Church of the Jericho Road Repairs

It is possible to be an expert in sin, to be able to discuss the crime, the alcohol, the drug problems in peoples' lives and not make any difference. There are people who can quote the statistics of environmental problems, nuclear threats, international threats and racial conflict. They can be prophets of doom and create feelings of fear and despair, but that is about all. The truly Christian church is different. It not only knows the tragedies and problems but it seeks to repair some of the brokenness that it has identified. Churches are doing that in many amazing and important ways. Because they see the need, they are

Providing warm lunches for the elderly
Staffing soup kitchens for the hungry
Developing thrift shops for the needy
Stocking food cupboards for poor people
Providing guidance in securing jobs for the unemployed
Encouraging their members to write letters to legislators
Giving after school care to latch key children
Visiting in nursing homes
Building homes through "Habitat for Humanity"
Grandparenting nursery school children
Building low-income housing
Building housing for the elderly
Visiting in prisons, nursing homes, hospitals
Providing services so older people can stay in their homes
Organizing remedial studies to compensate for inadequate
        public education

There is a biblical base for this in Jesus' description as we have it in Matthew 25. Those who will inherit the kingdom, he said, were those who gave food to the hungry, drink to the thirsty, a welcome to the stranger, clothing for the naked, and who visit the sick and those in prison. The person lying by the gutter on the Jericho Road had very specific and obvious needs. The Samaritan stopped to see what he could do. Jesus praised that.

The Church of the Jericho Road will deal with specific and critical needs. Needs are obvious to anyone who has imagination or sensitivity. In the Gospels Jesus talks about those who have these needs but in less physical or obvious ways. They are not physically in the gutter. We know them as hungry for affection, thirsty for understanding, lonely, scared about their vocational responsibilities, sick of life, drinking too much to avoid it and imprisoned within tortured memories of past sins.

One of our problems is that we are so accustomed to looking to government for solutions to life's problems that when the church gets involved some say, "Why are we doing that? Outpatient departments of hospitals, nursing homes, Alcoholics Anonymous and homes for unwed mothers all do these things." What is Christian about that? What is Christian indeed! First, it was the churches who originally founded hospitals, schools and other institutions in our society that meet human need. The fact is that society has so cut down on many of these resources that there are terrible voids. The other fact is that some of those dealing in the services "for profit" have little of the motivation or compassion of church people.

There is something exciting about meeting human need and feeling you make a difference. Whether it is handing food to a desperately hungry person or rocking a lonely pre-school child, it is obviously very important. Whatever government does or social agencies do, they either need to be kept honest to really meet needs, or supplemented by the service of caring people who will do it in the name of Jesus Christ.

The Samaritan went to the wounded man and bound up his wounds, pouring on oil and wine, sat him on his beast and took him to an inn and took care of him. The Church of the Jericho Road will go to the wounded and needy, will minister to their most obvious and special needs, and will see that they get the kind of attention that is appropriate to their situation. That church will test itself, not by what it can get in notoriety or size but by the magnitude of its heart and compassion in meeting the truly human need that is so much around us.

The Church of the Jericho Road Reorders

You know the old story of the ambulance at the bottom of the cliff, picking up the injured who fell over. Someone finally asked, "Why don't we build a fence at the top of the cliff so people won't fall off?"

There are systems in our society that are making people poor; rejecting them because of race, age or sex; preventing them from having adequate housing, a good education, adequate health care or meaningful work. For years, as things have changed quickly, different people have said that if the church doesn't offer theological guidance on important developing issues, the courts or the government will do so. Now we are faced with critically important decisions. The court and the government are determining our values and responses to

Surrogate motherhood
Organ transplants
Termination of life support systems
Disposal of nuclear waste
Racial standards and values

These are some of the developing issues. People in a local church are not equipped to provide definitive answers. But the issues are worth thinking and praying about. They are worth our attention and raising to visibility in our community. They are worth raising in a national debate. We can encourage our denomination to study and suggest values that can guide Christians in their response.

The church is the one place in society where big issues can be dealt with where there is no vested interest or personal profit to gain from suggestions or standards.

People in prisons and mental hospitals have few who will advocate for them. Christian people can raise fundamental questions in a society that figures that the response to crime is to build bigger prisons and give out longer sentences. Those of us who have been inside prisons know how abusive and impersonal they can be. We wonder that all prisoners do not come out with warped personalities and a driving desire to get even with society.

But the question we have to deal with is: WHY?

Why do people abuse drugs?
Why do people commit crimes?
Why do people become alcoholics?
Why do marriages break up?
Why do people abuse their spouses or children?
Why do nations see the military as the answer to complex
    international problems?
Why are so many homeless?
Why is there so much poverty?
What should we do about AIDS?

We cannot deal with all of these, but the Church of the Jericho Road will ask Jericho-Road-type questions. Why is that a dangerous road? Why are there people living along it who live lives of crime? What can society do to create situations that encourage people to live positive, useful lives?

Within the church we have special resources: public buildings and people. We can use those to affect public opinion and to develop relationships with other people who might share our search for a more humane society. Forums on local issues of interest might well lead to a community group actively dealing with a specific issue. Forums on subjects of special need can bring these to the attention of the public. Then the church might look for an area where it can work in the reordering of society. Welfare standards, inner-city education, peace concerns, justice in its broadest sense all demand a broad-based definition and theological description. These are difficult and complex issues which the church must understand. We have to put these in terms of our faith and know that they have to be dealt with over a long period of time. We know these are cancers infecting many human lives. They have to be dealt with so there will not be people needing immediate and emergency care. We know God works through us to affect the underlying nature of evil that destroys. We know God calls us to invest our energies to deal with the very roots of society and culture so that there will be new expectations concerning justice and positive attitudes toward resolving all that destroys and warps God's children.

Conclusion

As we read the book of Revelation we hear the Master saying:

> Behold, I stand at the door and knock; if anyone hears my voice and opens the door I will come in to him and eat with him and he with me.

The Church of the Jericho Road will be open to the Master and be a means through which the Lord can fulfill divine purposes. But the excitement and the joy that such relationships and such activities will engender make the church a place of anticipation and value. The church will be a place of imagination and excitement rather than dull and routine with little activity.

The Church of the Jericho Road is an experience of faith and change. Truly God is there! It's a church where the members choose each week to be there because they are eager to understand in new ways how to live on the Jericho Road. It is a church where we put together our best resources, our deep commitment to Jesus Christ and our discipleship as Christians. We will not be victims of this world, but molders of a caring society. We will not accept things as they are but seek to reflect the spirit of Jesus Christ in very specific ways that Christ might be honored and people's lives might be blessed.

Reverend Miles Jerome Jones

The Reverend Miles Jones pastors the Providence Park Baptist Church in Richmond, Virginia. Here he daily strives to connect the gospel with life. Serving as pastor since 1963, he and the members of Providence Park have made a significant impact on the Richmond community. They have believed the gospel, trusted that what seemed impossible to human eyes was indeed possible with God, and because they so believed, they lived to see some of the changes occur.

But Reverend Jones has not been content to simply shepherd the congregation at Providence Park. He has reached out to share God's vision with seminarians as adjunct faculty member of Virginia Union's School of Theology. Here, as teacher, he has challenged future ministers, struggled with colleagues, and deepened his own understandings of ministry.

Miles Jones is pastor, mentor, teacher, friend, one who is willing to believe the radicalness of the gospel and live it out.

Our Double Duty Destiny

by Miles Jerome Jones

While he was speaking, a Pharisee asked him to dine with him; so he went in and sat at the table. The Pharisee was astonished to see that he did not first wash before dinner. And the Lord said to him, "Now you Pharisees cleanse the outside of the cup and of the dish, but inside you are full of extortion and wickedness. You fools! Did not he who made the outside make the inside also? But give for alms those things which are within; and behold, everything is clean for you. But woe to you Pharisees! for you tithe mint and rue and every herb, and neglect justice and the love of God; these you ought to have done, without neglecting the others. Woe to you Pharisees! for you love the best seat in the synagogues and salutations in the market places. Woe to you; for you are like graves which are not seen and men walk over them without knowing it." (Luke 11:37–44)

I want to express my appreciation for the privilege that is mine to continue what has begun here today. This occasion is a significant one for me, as I am sure it is for all of us, because it brings together a combination of concerns. On the one hand the church is concerned with continuing its ministry to those of us who believe that Jesus Christ is Lord. And at the same time it is seeking ways by which that ministry can be expanded to include community concerns.

The church has a marvelous, thrilling challenge. This is an exciting time to see if the concerns of the church can be interpreted in the light of the community's interest and commend those who are here investigating and discussing and questioning and sharing and probing the relationship between the Christian faith and community needs. It's a promising endeavor. And so this opportunity that is ours further underscores the privilege that we have to be workers together in God's great vineyard.

The Scripture to which I draw your attention is taken from the eleventh chapter of Luke's Gospel. There is a sense in which it underscores what I would like to call our "Double Duty Destiny." There was an occasion when Jesus was about his ministry of teaching and preaching, beginning at the thirty-seventh verse of the eleventh chapter and continuing through the forty-fourth verse. He was asked by a Pharisee to come in and dine. So he went in and sat at table with the Pharisee. This religious leader was astonished to see that Jesus did not first wash before eating. And because the Pharisee obviously demonstrated his astonishment, Jesus said to him: "Now you Pharisees cleanse the outside of the cup and of the dish, but inside you are full of extortion and wickedness. You fools! Did not he who made the outside make the inside also? But give for alms those things which are within; and behold, everything is clean for you."

And then Jesus launched into what was for him uncharacteristically strong language. He began to berate the Pharisees, which is not usually like Jesus. He began to utter strong words of *woe*. When Jesus says "woe," that's a word of condemnation. He said:

> "But woe to you Pharisees! for you tithe mint and rue and every herb, and neglect justice and the love of God; these you ought to have done, without neglecting the others. Woe to you Pharisees! for you love the best seat in the synagogues and salutations in the market places. Woe to you; for you are like graves which are not seen, and men walk over them without knowing it."

This language, I say, is unlike Jesus, which means this must be important to him. It is uncharacteristic of our Lord to use such strong terms. Moreover, the importance of this incident must have stuck in the community of believers because not only is it recorded here, but Matthew's Gospel records it as well. That gives it a certain amount of importance. Recollection of his utterance seems to have impressed the early Christian community. For although all of his words were serious, these seem to be more so. Now we hear him using condemning words of woe which we do not often hear coming from his lips. We hear him speaking with scathing denunciation which is most unusual. What is the cause for such criticism from one who is renowned for compassion? What is it that prompts this kind of word from Jesus?

Let me hasten to say that the reason is wrapped up in the fact that these particular persons, the Pharisees, were those who gave leadership to the religious activities of their time and place. They were foremost in the religious establishment. We can call them "church members." If we dare refer to them in such language, they were stalwart members of the religious community. They were persons with whom you and I could readily identify. They were not aliens to church concerns. They were not outsiders. They were those who said their prayers with regularity, and ritualistically underwent those tasks associated with religious emphasis. Oh, it was a different time to be sure, but they were about the same kind of thing in which you and I become engaged—providing leadership in religious affairs.

Jesus has a word for them and us. His word is wrapped up in the fact that these persons have not fulfilled the requirements of their particularity. That is, they have neglected an important part of their responsibility as unique representatives of the Eternal. While it is true they were scrupulously careful in their tithing, scrupulously careful in their contributions, scrupulously careful in their religiosity, scrupulously careful in what they did to gain high regard in the religious establishment, they were at the same time woefully neglectful in their practice of personal relationship to God.

This evoked strong words from Jesus. Now he does not say they should stop doing anything. He does not say, "You should not have done that." Rather, he says, "This you should have done. You should be scrupulously circumspect about your religious traditions. You should be concerned about how you go about your churchly affairs. This you should have done . . . without neglecting the other." It is this neglect of the other that seems to arouse his indignation. He is concerned about that part of the responsibility left undone. It's their unwillingness, their inability to link "this" with "that," which concerns Jesus. It's their inability to see that theirs is a double duty destiny. It's their lack of double duty vision that arouses in him such heightened indignation because they have failed to see "this you should have done without leaving the other undone."

Now we, you and I, are accustomed to being condemned for what we do. We do many things we should not do. We have to acknowledge that. We do many things we have no business doing and sometimes we're sorry for doing them. If we received condemnation from the Eternal we'd understand because we know we had no business doing those things. Some things we do, we shouldn't, and if we are chastised or criticized we understand why. But this is different. Jesus is not saying you should not have done this. He says do this—you're doing all right. The criticism is failure to do *that*. You do not see your duty in dual terms!

Now what might this mean for us? Can we tuck this away somewhere in the eleventh chapter of the Gospel of Luke and leave it there? Is this word for you and for me where we sit and where we worship and where we live? Does it say anything at all about what we are about here, now, tonight in this place? How about this week in the endeavor in which we are engaged? Does it speak to us, or is this word confined to the Pharisees? Is this just Jesus' way of being outspoken and condemning and critical? Is he just speaking in these critical terms to make his point for them?

I agree with you. "No! No!" You say, "No!" and I say "No!" because we know this word is not confined to a particular time or place. This is something intuitive about us. We know this is our word too. What might Jesus be saying to us? What could this mean to us? Given the circumstances of our being, given the concerns of our interests tonight, what might it mean to us?

Is it possible you and I tend sometimes to overlook the double duty nature of our relationship? We are not condemned for our concern about individualistic soul-saving. That's good. We ought to be engaged in the endeavor of evangelism to win individuals to Christ. I believe he would say that's all right. I believe there's merit in revivals that seek to win converts to Christ. I think there is merit in seeking to gain those whom we call sinners into the church. We ought to do that. I don't think that is wrong nor do I think that Jesus would say that it's wrong. But I believe at the same time you and I need to understand the double dimensions of our duty.

Do we need to remember that the religious enterprise might also include a dimension that we sometimes tend to overlook? There is a community concern that also needs our attention. It's not just saving souls—as important as that is—this we ought to have done; but it's saving cities, individuals *and* communities, persons and environments. This, too, we ought to have done and ought to do. For the sake of everything Jesus said, for the sake of his word that we ought to hear, *don't leave this undone!*

Having heard Jesus' word, our task, yours and mine under God, is to do both *this* and *that;* for he gives substantive meaning to what might have been no more than a pronoun in my previous concern. Now, it is to do *this* without leaving *that* undone.

I think God would have us be resourceful in helping folk link *this* with *that* because I believe it finds its root and meaning in who the Christ was. He was himself the link. The reason he could speak with strong language is because of who he was. He could talk like that because He is the link between *this* and *that.* He hooks up every *this* with every *that* and he begins to unite the human and the divine, the high and the low. In him one finds the link of life. He's the link, and if you ever want to "get it together," in any way, resort to him. He'll help you hook up your *this* and *that,* and he does it in such a marvelous way. I like the way he helps us do that.

What will Jesus do for us and for our concern about caring

for our communities? Jesus will help us do *this*, namely care for individuals by inviting them to find their salvation in him. Jesus will strengthen our efforts at evangelism, as we seek out those who are lost and introduce them to him. But, Jesus will also help us do *that*, namely care for communities where people are lost in poverty and degradation and need. Jesus will strengthen our efforts at community development as we seek to help people find new hope who are deprived and victimized. I am talking about fulfillment.

Fulfillment consists of both *this* and *that*. Fulfillment is both these things and those. It's always keeping *this* related to *that*. The danger is separating these things from those things. You know, I believe that ever since Adam made his mistake in the garden the problem with life has been disassociating, cutting-off, alienating and separating. That which ought to be one got separated and ever since Eden the activity of the Eternal has been in overcoming the separation. That which ought to be together we keep separated.

Two is not bad. Two is all right. But that which ought to be one ought to be together. The way God has got the world purposely created means fulfillment comes about when separation is overcome and unity is affirmed. In other words, when *this* can be related to *that;* when someone can bridge the gap and overcome the chasm.

There is real justification for linking *this* with *that* and the justification is theological. It is rooted and grounded in what God is doing. It is not just sociological. It's not simply the idea of our wanting to do things together so they look good. There is a fundamental unity at the heart of creation which God has put at the center of everything we are called to do. There is a unity here which we must affirm and to separate is to distort.

That's what Jesus was saying. To separate what ought to be united is to distort reality. It is to divide things so badly that they are out of focus. And so Jesus says to the Pharisees, "Woe to you. You ought to know better!" You people of the religious persuasion ought to understand the Divine intention. Woe to you. Let other folk misunderstand it; but you who are religious, woe to you! You are condemned. If you don't understand *this* with *that* you're doing something alien to the will of God. Whenever you overcome what we would normally classify as distinctions and differences and chasms and separations, you are doing God's business. If ever you can find any way you can get the "economic ups" and "social downs" together, if you ever find some way of getting the folk on *that* side of town with the folk on *this* side of town, you are about God's business. If you find some way of overcoming the chasms we construct, you are doing God's business. If ever in our nation we find some way of bridging the gap and bringing black and white together, we then will be about God's business, and we will have moved from present postures of desegregation to the degree of integration that was envisioned by persons like Martin Luther King, Jr.

I want to identify why I think there are some real possibilities in this word of Scripture. The text begins by saying that the Pharisee invited Jesus in to dinner, after which the conversation started. We can invite Jesus in to dinner, as it were, and still not discern the depth of what He is about. We can invite him into our house, into our lives, into our church and yet not discern the depth of Jesus' concerns. This same Pharisee who invited Jesus in was critical of Jesus when he got there. He didn't understand the Master. He invited him into his house and yet indicated astonishment because of nontraditional behavior. And sometimes we too are guilty of that kind of misunderstanding when we do not see him for who he really is. He is, I repeat, the link between *this* and *that.*

This is what we ought to have done and *that* is what we have neglected to do. He is the one who can bridge the gap. Let us today resolve to overcome the separation that exists between what we are doing in church and ought to be doing in communities. As individuals, as a church, as a community and as a congregation, let us want to overcome the gap. Let us want to be about doing both *this* and *that.*

Do you know you can affirm unity today? Do you know you can overcome the chasm today? Do you know that as a consequence of our having heard the word today, in your individual life and in your collective life, you can overcome the gap, the chasm? He provides unity. By all means, do as the Pharisee and invite him in, but let him make a difference when He gets in!

The Reverend Doctor Keith Russell

Keith Russell is the president of New York Theological Seminary. He has been pastor of the Grace Baptist Church in the Bronx, Emmanuel Baptist Church in Albany and Baptist Church of the Redeemer in Brooklyn.

He has spent most of his ministry helping congregations confront the needs of their neighborhoods while seeking to increase the participation and cooperation of Christian congregations and denominations.

How Ministry Shapes the Church

by Keith Russell

> When John's disciples told him about all these things, he called two of them and sent them to the Lord to ask him, "Are you the one John said was going to come, or should we expect someone else?"
> When they came to Jesus, they said, "John the Baptist sent us to ask if you are the one he said was going to come, or should we expect someone else?"
> At that very time Jesus healed many people from their sicknesses, diseases, and evil spirits, and gave sight to many blind people. He answered John's messengers, "Go back and tell John what you have seen and heard: the blind can see, the lame can walk, those who suffer from dreaded skin diseases are made clean, the deaf can hear, the dead are raised to life, and the Good News is preached to the poor. How happy are those who have no doubts about me!" (Luke 7:18–23, TEV)

In the Gospel of Luke, chapter 7, verses 18-23, we find John the Baptist in prison. While in prison, John is beginning to have second thoughts about the authenticity of this man named Jesus. His second thoughts are so severe that he sends his disciples to Jesus and they ask Jesus, "Are you the one or should we look to another?" Jesus responds to this question by saying to John's disciples, "Go tell John what you hear and what you see. Go tell John the blind see, the deaf hear, the lame walk, the lepers are cleansed, the dead are raised and the poor

I would like to begin the exploration of the question of how ministry shapes the church by suggesting that this story of the interaction between Jesus and John provides the ingredients to define both the church and ministry. From this story the church is nothing more and nothing less than a community of people who abide in the presence of the Messiah and who practice the same ministry the Messiah practices. The church is that community of believers who, living in messianic power, perform messianic ministry. The church is defined by its ministry and recognized as being faithful to Jesus by the work it does.

What is this ministry? The ministry is that of healing, proclaiming, raising up the dead and calling forth life. It is anointing, proclaiming good news, liberating the oppressed, taking no offense at him who is in fact Lord of lords and King of kings. In other words, the church is recognized as a messianic community not by what it says but by what it does. Simply put, the ministry is the practice of the Messiah's own ministry, and it is in that sense that the church, when faithful, finds its ministry in the very ministry of Jesus.

This means that the church does not, when faithful, shape its own ministry. The church does not design, create or manufacture its own ministry. Rather, the church is shaped by ministry. The church is given a ministry and it is to organize itself, form itself, train itself, equip itself around the task of ministry to which it is called. The church does not shape its own ministry; it is shaped by the ministry which is given to it by virtue of its being a community of Messiah-believing, Messiah-practicing men and women.

I must hasten to say that far too often the church is not shaped by its ministry and tries simply to be one that designs, organizes and creates ministry. Far too often the church is shaped more by the behavior of the world in which it lives, the attitudes of success and power of the culture, the wealth or influence of its membership, than by the central ministry practiced by the Messiah. Frequently the church is shaped by the world and plays at ministry. I am calling for a critical investigation of how ministry shapes the church so that the church, in its very form and function, reflects the tasks to which it is called.

There are several key elements which allow ministry to shape the church. The first is the understanding of a "call." I believe that God, through the power of the Holy Spirit, continues to work in history in our time calling specific congregations of people to engage in specific tasks of ministry. That is, God asks people to proclaim the Word. God raises up people who are healers. God calls congregations and communities to engage in liberating practice. God calls communities of Christians to feed the poor, to house the outcasts, to minister to the oppressed. God continues to call. When a call is heard churches organize themselves around that calling. When a divine mandate is given, a church has no choice except to take its time, its money, its energy, its resources and to give them to that mandate. Ministry does not shape the church unless the church is in touch with the profound and powerful sense of God's call. The fact that many churches are not shaped by ministry simply indicates that many churches are no longer in touch with the call. Certainly they practice what they have historically practiced, but there is no deep sense of power, or energy, or life surging through the body of believers. Such churches end up trying to shape ministry. What I am calling for is the ministry to shape the church; and a key critical element in the shaping of the church is the call that God gives to the ministry God wants performed.

The second element following closely upon the call is the task of recognizing and using gifts. Too often the church leaves ministry to the professionals—to the pastors, to those who have been "trained." When a call is heard, gifts are called forth. As gifts are called forth, they must be both recognized and utilized. The church, the community of Messiah believers, must as a body both perceive the call and use the variety of gifts that God has given it to perform the task to which it is called. The fact that there is so little activity in so many churches simply reflects that a call hasn't been heard and that gifts are not being utilized. As long as ministry is the minister's job, the church is not shaped by ministry, it is simply avoiding it. Ministry will not become central to the church's function until the members of the body experience the terms of the call and begin to discern the gifts which the Spirit has given.

A key to the future of the church is the recovery of the gifts of the people. The people of God, men and women who belong to the church, must perceive the essential importance of living out their gifts in light of the call to which they have been called. When gifts are discerned, men and women become hungry to be trained, to be equipped, to use those gifts. Those gifts are needed to fulfill the divine mandate which God has given. When that begins to happen, ministry is shaping the very life of the church and the church moves from being simply a body which reacts to a body which interacts with the power of God as it makes itself known in the world. One must be called, yes, and one must discern gifts, yes, but one must, after all, practice what the call requires.

Another key element in allowing ministry to shape the church is to put into concrete practice what God is asking to be done. Now that sounds simple and yet it is quite difficult. For I have heard many pastors and many church people tell me that they would like to do what God wants, but they do not have enough money; or, they do not have enough people; or, they do not have enough gifts; or, they do not have enough resources; or, they do not have enough fresh ideas. The key to allowing ministry to shape the church is to do what God asks one to do and to trust that as one enters in the doing of ministry, the resources will follow right along. The key to allowing ministry to shape the church is the concrete practice of ministry. If God asks you to proclaim, proclaim; if to heal, heal; if to cast out, cast out; if to confront demons, confront demons; if to release the oppressed, release the oppressed. For ministry shapes the church to the degree to which ministry becomes the sum and substance of the church's reason for existence.

One can tell if ministry is the church's reason to exist in any church, anywhere in this country, simply by looking at what the church does. Does the church practice being the community of Messiah believers? Does the church practice what the Messiah practiced? Is there something happening in the life of that church which shows good news, which bespeaks healing and health, which symbolizes the power of God over sin, which symbolizes the power of God to create new life? Are there, in the church's shape, in the church's function, in the church's very life, signs of the practice of the messianic ministry? Clearly, if ministry is to shape the life of the church, it will show itself in what the church does or does not do. A called church, a church working at discerning its gifts and equipping its saints, will sooner or later show forth that understanding, that calling, that equipping in concrete practice; and that concrete practice will spill out into the streets and highways and byways of this time.

Having tried to develop a framework for understanding how ministry shapes the church, let me now illustrate these dynamics. First, consider a church which began to experience a call developing in relationship to caring for persons recently released from state mental hospitals. A significant number of former patients of these hospitals were finding their way to the streets of the city and were not being adequately cared for. This church began to sense that they had both opportunity and resources to begin caring for and ministering to this group of people. Cooperating with other agencies, they began to open the doors of their building to these people. People began to respond to this invitation and to socialization.

Soon, however, a problem became clear. This group of people, generally, were heavy smokers. The church had a rule forbidding smoking on its premises. Now came the critical time of decision. Would ministry shape the church or would the church attempt to shape its ministry? That is, would this church allow the needs of its new ministry to shape its form and function or would it attempt to have these new persons who were the center of its ministry be constricted and controlled by its rules and regulations? The church struggled with its rules *versus* the needs of this new ministry and decided that the needs of these persons, as well as the opportunity to minister to them, was more important than enforcing the rule about smoking. The church discovered that when they are called to ministry, the ministry has a way of shaping the church. This ministry meant that they had to rethink and reestablish the practices of their building use in order to be effectively sensitive to this new group of people that God had sent them. When faced with the call of ministry, the church changed its shape and allowed the new ministry to begin affecting its form and function.

For a second example consider the illustration of another church which found itself located in a community that was becoming increasingly multicultural. This predominantly white church discovered that in the community surrounding their building new groups of people were locating themselves. In this community there were increasing numbers of people representing various and diverse cultural groups. The church was surrounded by Asian, Hispanic, Haitian, West Indian and American black cultures. The church members began to know that God was calling them to open their doors to the community as it was developing. They began to respond to what they perceived to be God's call by inviting these ethnic groups to become part of their church ministry. As the invitation was made, more and more groups and persons responded. After a short period of time this once predominantly white church began to reflect the nature of its community. More and more of the residents began to participate in the life of the church.

Now a problem presents itself. As a church begins to broaden its life and increase its numbers, who continues to have the dominant control of the church? Here again we are faced with the question of whether the church will try to form and shape its own ministry. Frequently when churches go through racial transition the dominant original group seeks to keep control of building resources and decision making. That attempt to control is a reflection of how often the church tries to shape ministry. But when ministry shapes the church new forms of participation, a sharing of power and the broadening of decision making is required.

The ministry of including and creating a multicultural community brings with it a new shape of decision making, resource sharing and new forms of leadership. This particular church was faced with the question of whether its new outreach would be reflected in how it internally ran itself. Would the original members continue to hold on to the power and the resources, or would the power and resources of the church begin to be shared? Would the church allow leadership to emerge from the newer participants in its ministry? Here again is an example of a church at the crossroad, deciding whether they would allow the new call to shape what the church would become, or whether they would try to take the church and control the ministry as it developed.

This particular church slowly and with some pain allowed the ministry of the developing multicultural Christian community to shape it. Rather than trying to control they began to allow the church, as it was emerging, to develop leadership, participate in decision making, and form the basis of a new and broader community. So often the opposite is just the case. Too often the church feels called to reach out but tries to control and shape the reaching out in such a way that what results is a kind of paternalistic racism which keeps those who were in control in control. This congregation wrestled with the call of a ministry and responded to the call of allowing it to produce a new shape and a new form in this ministry as it was developed.

As you examine the current life of your church, what do you conclude about the role that ministry plays in shaping it? Can one tell that ministry is shaping the emerging form of your church by looking at what your church does? Remember the story with which we began. We are called to be a community of Messiah servants and to participate in the same activity in which the Messiah participated. Whether your church is allowing ministry to shape it can be seen when one asks if, as a result of your life, the blind are seeing, the lame are walking, the dead are being raised, and the poor are having good news preached to them. Is the dynamic life-giving power of Jesus shaping the response, the activity, and the life of your church?

The church does not have the right to shape its ministry if it is truly the church. The true church is always formed and shaped by the ministry to which it is called. How is it in the church to which you belong?

Let me conclude by asking three questions: First, is ministry shaping your church? Second, is a call to ministry bringing forth your gifts and organizing your resources? Third, what does the practice of your church suggest about your ministry?

The Reverend Yamina Apolinaris

Yamina Apolinaris, an ordained American Baptist minister, is program manager of the Urban Strategy Development Program for the Board of National Ministries, ABC/USA. A graduate of Andover Newton Theological School, she was the first woman with theological training to be called to the pastorate among the Baptist Churches of Puerto Rico. She was also the first woman president of the Baptist Churches of Puerto Rico.

To Be with Christ In the World

by Yamina Apolinaris

Jesus went up into the hills and called to him those he wanted, and they came to him. He appointed twelve—designating them apostles—that they might be with him.... (Mark 3:13-14, NIV)

The passage that I am using as a basis for reflection is one of the accounts of the calling of the disciples. It is my understanding that this narrative is not an actual description of how and when the calling of the disciples took place, but rather an affirmation of the tradition of the Twelve; those that were recognized as eyewitnesses of Jesus' ministry, and apostles commissioned to carry out his work.

This narrative from Mark is different from that of Matthew and Luke, particularly in the introduction. As I look at the passage, two concerns seem to be underlying Mark's introduction:

1. Why was this particular group chosen from Jesus' followers to be his disciples?
2. What was the meaning/significance of that call?

Although I want to focus our attention on the second concern, there are a few things I would like to share regarding the first question. Why was this particular group chosen? Mark's answer is very simple. "Jesus called those whom he wanted and they came to him." I am sure the question regarding the election of the disciples came up with some frequency at the discussions of the early Christian communities. It certainly has been a topic in our discussions, too. Why those twelve?

In the Gospels little effort is put into portraying the disciples as good collaborators to Jesus' ministry. Very often their presence proved to be more of an obstacle than a help. And yet, here they are, carrying on the ministry. That very ministry they seemed not always to have understood.

Mark's answer might look to some as an evasion of the issues, but not to me. The statement is not dealing with the issue of rejection of those who were not called, but the affirmation of the ones who were. I can't help but think of the time when I was growing up in Puerto Rico. We used to play on teams. And every team had a "captain" whose main role was to choose the players. Very often I had to go through the experience of being the last one to be called. How many times I had to stand alone while two captains argued over who had the bad luck to have me on their team! There is nothing like being rejected because one does not meet the standards.

Jesus chose those whom he wanted with no specific qualifications, no lists of special abilities, gifts or accomplishments. Jesus called those whom he wanted and they came to him. The passage reminds us, today, that Jesus is still calling those whom he wants regardless of their sex, age, ethnic background or accent. The only requirement is the willingness to come to him. The willingness to put one's life in God's hands, to take that step, is the only requirement. Jesus called and the disciples responded. Were they reluctant? joyful? scared to death? The text doesn't say. They just came to him.

But as I said at the beginning, Mark is also dealing with another question: The issue of the meaning and significance of that call.

> He chose twelve, so they could be with him . . . to send them out to preach, and to have power to heal and cast out demons. (Mark 3:14, paraphrased).

He established twelve to be with him—to be with Christ. How can we interpret this? In what ways can the mere "being" with Christ help these disciples who had to carry on the ministry without the physical presence of their teacher? What is it that Mark is trying to tell us?

I came from a tradition that has defined "being with Christ" mostly in spiritual terms. We go to church to be with Christ. We go to retreats to be with Christ. Hymns such as "I Come to the Garden Alone" and "Apart from the World" are examples of the emphasis we've placed on an individualistic relationship with God. And yet, when we listen to Mark, we cannot believe that Mark was defining "being with Christ" in merely spiritual terms.

As a way to motivate your thinking I will make just two affirmations: First, being with Christ places the disciples closer to people and to the world. The gospel gives testimony to Christ, the one who was and is always *present*. The effectiveness of Jesus' ministry lies in the fact that he was always present, within reach.

Let us turn to the narrative of Jesus' encounter with the leper. Categories of the sacred and the profane, clean and unclean, were very clear in the priestly tradition. The leper was estranged from the community of the clean for he or she was considered to be under God's judgment and punishment. The leper was an untouchable. They even had to go around saying, "I am unclean. I am unclean," so that no one could get close to them. It was not chance or mistake that placed Jesus within reach of the lepers. Jesus made himself available. He entered the territory of the leper.

Long before my family could afford to buy a television, we used to go to the center of Old San Juan, to the place where there was a public television. People who worked close by or who just happened to be shopping or visiting would gather at the television for coffee break or lunch. The ones who lived closer by would come at night for some evening entertainment. The first time I sat in front of my own television to watch some religious program and saw this person who was very well dressed, clean, sharp saying you must send us your contributions so that we may be able to survive, I thought about those men and women, sitting on the cement benches at the plaza, eating a bowl of rice and beans or drinking their coffee and bread because this was the only thing they could afford. Let's talk about survival!

I've seen patients gathered around a television set at the hospital lounge, escaping for a moment from the pain, the cries, the smells. They were listening to someone say, "Jesus loves you and so do we." But that someone looked like he or she had never been sick. That person looked like someone who had never experienced what it is to lie awake all night long because the cry of the person next to you reminds you of your own pain. What is it to feel alone and forsaken by God?

I'm not saying that television or other media cannot be effective in our ministries; indeed they are. What I am saying is that they can never be substitutes for our own touch, warmth, presence.

It's so easy to fall into the temptation to stay at a distance. We don't get dirty that way. Staying at a distance doesn't require any effort. We don't run the risk of making mistakes. We don't get headaches. It is so easy to stay in that safe and comfortable space in our office, our congregation, the cubicle of friends and acquaintances, the safety of our own spiritual world. At a distance both the images we project as well as the ones that we receive are distorted. Jesus called the disciples to be with him, to take them to the people whose needs had to be met. Even today to respond to Christ's call is to be willing to accompany Jesus, entering the territory of the so-called lepers of our time. To be with Christ is to recognize Christ's face in the lives of the poor, the alienated, the sick, the troubled, the needy, the rejected, the little ones who surround us.

The second affirmation I make is that Jesus called the disciples to be with him, but he also called them to send them out to preach and to heal and to cast out demons. What a powerful image this is. This makes the call so complete and wholistic. Not only are they called to be present, but to *do* something

Disciples are called to overturn the fixed order of this world, to proclaim a word that could open the door for creation/changes/new possibilities. Disciples are called to say to the lonely, the weak, the defenseless, the oppressed, "God is present and at work on your behalf."

Let's return to the story of the leper. Upon entering the territory of the leper, Jesus was confronted. The leper said, "If you want you can heal me." At first hearing these words seem to be the pleading of one who feels at the mercy of a stronger person. But if we listen closely we will discover the leper is actually challenging Jesus.

"If you want you can heal me." The leper is reminding Jesus that he has the power to change the leper's condition. The leper is reminding Jesus—more than that, challenging Jesus—to do what he was sent out to accomplish. "You can do something. Well do it!" And Jesus responds. Jesus recognized that the claim of the leper is legitimate, valid. Jesus cannot do otherwise than to respond.

In talking about justice and love, Reinhold Niebuhr said:

> Philanthropy is giving to those who make claims against us, who do not challenge our goodness or disinterestedness. An act of philanthropy may thus be an expression of both power and moral complacency. An act of justice, on the other hand, requires the humble recognition that the claim that another makes against us may be legitimate.[1]

You and I, all of us, need to be reminded over and over again that indeed we have been called—that Christ has called us to be with him, and that being with Christ will place us in the territory of those who have been rejected, alienated, stamped as lepers. We have been called not just to be present for philanthropic purposes, but beyond that to respond to the claims of our brothers and sisters in need.

Preach good news, the good news that God's reign is here, a reign of justice. Heal the wounds of those who are hurt, so that

---

[1]Reinhold Niebuhr, *Love and Justice: Selections from the Shorter Writings of Reinhold Niebuhr,* ed. D.B. Robertson (Magnolia, Mass.: Peter Smith Publisher Inc., n.d.).

they can stand and walk again. Feed the hungry so that they may have strength. Dress the naked so that they may walk with dignity. Cast out the demons. Get involved in systemic changes. Work toward the changes in attitudes and work toward freeing the oppressed and oppressors.

Jesus called those whom he wanted to be with him and he gave them power to proclaim and to serve, to heal and restore. Jesus called those whom he wanted. We, too, have been called.

Reverend James C. Miller

Rev. James C. Miller has been pastor of the Lake Avenue Baptist Church since 1980. Previous pastorates include First Baptist, Worcester, Mass.; Emmanuel Baptist, Schenectady, N.Y.; and First Baptist, Cooperstown, N.Y.

He is a graduate of Alderson Broaddus College in West Virginia and Colgate-Rochester Divinity School in New York. He has served in numerous denominational and ecumenical positions, the most recent as chairperson for the Commission on Life and Theology. He is on the board of the Urban League of Rochester.

His community activities involve developing new community strategies and initiating new urban ministries programs.

He helped begin the Ministry of the Laity project at Andover Newtown Theological School.

Defrost Your Frozen Assets[1]

by James C. Miller

> Do not be conformed to this world but be transformed by the renewal of your mind, that you may prove what is the will of God, what is good and acceptable and perfect. (Romans 12:2)

When I selected my sermon title a week ago, little did I know that New England would experience its worst blizzard in years. The sermon title was prompted by a newspaper article that described a huge building gutted by fire. The irony of the story is the building was an ice warehouse that contained thousands of tons of block ice held in storage. The writer of the newspaper article called attention to the fact that although the building had actually contained thousands of gallons of potential extinguisher, it was not in available form. Frozen assets!

A similar tragedy is suffered in our churches, our families, institutions, communities, even our personal lives—there are plenty of assets, a magnitude of talent, a commanding expertise of knowledge; but we seem unable to command it, to have it at our disposal in the right form when we need the assets in available, usable form. Potential of all kinds is in and about us, but frozen.

One of my friends serves as executive secretary to Governor Jay Rockefeller of West Virginia. It is rumored in the Appalachian valleys that Governor Rockefeller's personal wealth, if distributed to him on a daily basis, is about $19,000. Yet, his secretary often pays for his coffee at informal coffee breaks, for he has not bothered to get some loose change, like quarters, dimes and nickels. $19,000 a day is not available in usable cash.

The same is true of assets and capabilities elsewhere. We want peace in the world, but most of our technical and economic genius is poured into war. We have technical capabilities to launch satellites that hover over Russia, Red China or Chile, and they are capable of beaming surveillance pictures to such detail that a human person can be recognized entering and leaving an embassy; yet, our police departments on the ground cannot focus on the persons who control the profitable and exploitive drug markets in America.

We have the assets but they do not seem to be in available forms for the right purpose. Assets are frozen, like the tons of caked ice in the warehouse that burned to the ground.

"Frozen assets" describes the dilemmas of the churches today. We have so much creative power; so many good brains; effective people with talent, education and experience; yet we often seem powerless and ineffective.

Mark Gibbs and Ralph Morton, two British theologians and ecumenists, analyze the contemporary church and conclude that we are God's frozen people! Their epitaph is based on a statement by the famous Dutch theologian, Hendrik Kraemer, which says, "In all our criticism and sometimes near despair of the institutional church, it should never be forgotten that many powers and possibilities really exist in it, but often in captivity, exist as frozen credits and dead capital."[2]

Kraemer's words are about the laity of the church. Laity, a beautiful word, is derived from a Greek term *laos*, which means the whole people of God. For some reason, you and I are often frozen when it comes to knowing and doing God's will in God's world. Though endowed with living power and creative possibilities, we exist as dead capital and frozen assets.

What is it that causes us to exist as if we are God's frozen people? What will it take to defrost our frozen assets?

First, a commanding belief that God has a high calling for your life will defrost your frozen assets.

If there is one particular word that I want you to know and get in touch with, it is the word "calling." To be called means to be summoned—directed, inspired, sent, placed—for a purpose, meaning, action, job, mission.

The task is to be God's human agent. Calling is to be obedient to do what you understand God wants done in a particular place. Calling is to understand what you can do to help others discern, experience and respond to God's love and reconciliation. Calling is to understand that God wishes to disclose love and reconciliation through you by the manner in which you live, work and love.

Richard Broholm, a remarkable human being and consultant who is working with our church in a strategy of ministry of the laity, has just concluded a survey funded by the United Methodist Church. His task was to see if women and men truly believe that they have a ministry that is inspired and informed by the church. Do church folk believe they are God's partners and interpreters in their daily work? The mounting evidence from Mr. Broholm's sampling is this: the vast majority of church members—God's people—hold no understanding that what they do in their daily work is based on a conviction that they are called to their positions by God. In addition, and even more sad, even if they do believe that their lives are an intentional partnership with God, they are of the opinion that the organized church really does not validate and support their daily routine as being a ministry for others that is honored and encouraged.

A few weeks ago the guardian of my children, a General Electric Company engineer, was prayed for and commissioned by his church for a business trip to the Soviet Union. Upon hearing of this commissioning service, his startled colleagues, who were also church members elsewhere, exclaimed, "I didn't know that the trip was going to be that dangerous!" All the local church was saying to Tom was: be sensitive to the ways that God intends to use your technical skills and human lifestyle; but colleagues saw the act as being something akin to "flight insurance."

I know Tom, and he sees his identity as an electrical engineer, a husband, a citizen, an agent of the General Electric Company, but deeper still, he sees his role as an agent of God, a member of the human family, a citizen of the kingdom of God, a person in whom and through whom God chooses to witness. It is this understanding of vocation, personal identity and mission in life which keeps Tom's living assets unfrozen.

I repeat, a commanding vision of your life ought to be this: You are called. You are chosen. You are placed in a particular arena for specific tasks—to do ministry for a particular God.

Do you believe what you are doing and how you are living are in any way related to God?

I share my conviction: I now have and have had several problems in life that are of major proportion. One problem which I have not yet encountered is a lack of understanding of how and where God wants to use my life. This is not because I am a clergyperson and, therefore, have a special pipeline to God's will for my life. I am convinced that if I were an attorney, a senator, a professor, an industrial community relations manager, a physician, a plumber—I would do those jobs knowing that God has given me a set of skills and placed me in one of those vocational arenas.

Presently I see God using my life as a professional person trained for ministry as a clergyperson. My mother saw her life used with the same validity by God as a salesperson in a department store and as a manager of a theater. Mark Hatfield sees himself as a minister working in the United States Senate. This week in Washington, Chuck Colson told the Religious Broadcasting Commission that he views his life as an attorney working for prison reform. I have no doubt but what my wife viewed her life not primarily as a minister's wife but a minister being a homemaker, teaching and caring for children.

The scriptural injunction from Romans 12:1-2 seems clear to me. "Do not be conformed to this world but be transformed by the renewal of your mind, that you may prove what is the will of God, what is good and acceptable and perfect."

Second, it is very possible, and I hope it is true, that you understand vocation to be a calling. Yet, you still feel frozen. Then the question might be for you: Do you have a commanding vision for your life that you are prepared to act on?

One of my favorite biblical texts is: "Unless the people have vision, they will perish" (Proverbs 29:18).

You and I may understand that we are called by God; but unless the calling is energized by a renewing vision, our lives are stale and insipid, like day-old ginger ale that has been uncorked. There is no fizz.

A lot of people lack vision. They seem complacent. They are standing still and the quickest way to freeze is to stand still. Ask any boy scout who hikes or soldier who has stood on military guard and they will tell you that a good hiker or sentry does not stand still if it is cold.

One becomes frozen gradually, almost without realizing it. What is your vision? What are your wishes for life? Can you look at the humdrum stuff you do every day and see in your ministries that you are enacting a vision for life? Management consultant Peter Drucker says, "There are no boring jobs, only bored, uninspired people working on those jobs." It is an old story, but forever true, I believe. Three separate workers at the same site were asked what they were doing. One worker replied, "I am digging a ditch." The second said, "I am building a multi-story structure." The third responded, "I, sir, am building a cathedral."

Third, if you lack a sense of calling, and if you lack a gripping vision, perhaps it is because you lack a commanding commitment to a person.

Some do not know Christ, or if they know him, they choose to shun any commitment to his call. The story is told of the man who was asked, "If your wife urged you to go out and look for work, what would you look for?" His reply: "A new wife." Too often when God urges us to get into the world and take up the work to be done, we want to look for a new god.

Scripture says, "present your bodies as a living sacrifice" (Romans 12:1). Jitsuo Morikawa, preaching as interim senior minister of the Riverside Church in New York City, spoke eloquently but bluntly to the congregation:

Life is for sacrifice, not for security. Life is for offering, not for feasting. Life is for the altar, not for the sewer. Life is for ministry, not self-serving. Life is not private ownership, placed on the market for the highest bidder, engaging in the business of the free enterprise system out of one's absolute freedom. Don't be deceived by ideologies of freedom, who pride themselves in the free enterprise system, by delusions of freedom and absolute rights of the individual. You don't have absolute individual rights. Absolute rights belong only to God, and you belong to God; you are his creation and creature, made in his image, inescapably his, under the authority and ultimate sovereignty of his will and his purpose. You are not free, ultimately free; you have no absolute freedom, only freedom within the bounds of God's authority and will, and when freedom is exercised outside of his will and authority, you do so to your own destruction. You are not free agents to sell yourselves and your services to the highest bidder; you belong to the ultimate owner of your soul; "you are not your own, you were bought with a price" (1 Cor. 6:19–20). You were ransomed, bonded and set free, by a high ransom payment.

I very much wish that I could help many of you with encouragement and support as to how you can lock yourself into a deeper and more personal commitment to Christ, Lord of the church and world. I believe that when you are tied to a living relationship with God, that calling and vision are fundamental gifts given to you. Christ's call to his first disciples was a person-to-person call. They were not called to believe a doctrine or to worship in a prescribed way. Fundamentally, they were called to trust Jesus and follow him. The early disciples were not people who could be considered "spiritual types," those who naturally enjoyed prayer, meditation and the aesthetics of worship. Instead, Jesus called people who were virile, earthy, involved in the routineness of life. They were the laity.

How odd that no time limit was implied in their original call.

He didn't ask them to sign up for a six-week course. When most of them started to follow Jesus, they could not have known that it was to be a lifetime call, but such is the persuasion and power of Jesus.

A remarkable executive of a major, private foundation and one who has been a pioneer in working with the United Nations in underdeveloped countries, has used his Christian faith to literally change the conditions of thousands and has personally communicated a sound faith in Jesus Christ to scores of associates. He tells an incredible story of his original call. Intrigued by a group of Christians and dissatisfied with much of his own life, he was at first frightened and then resistant to enter into a totality of Christian commitment. One of his friends asked him if he would consider turning his life over to Christ's management and direction for a one-week trial. "That's too long," was the reply. "How about one day?" "Can't do it," he retorted." "How about one hour?" Hesitantly, the executive said "Yes." And you can guess the rest. Since that moment he has not lived life on the old terms.

Defrost your frozen assets. Present your bodies as a living sacrifice. Sacrifice in the Old Testament was a burnt offering. Life must be enflamed, offered on the altars of the world's marketplaces, for in the world God establishes the altars where love and reconciliation are to be exchanged for obedience and devotion.

[1]Title taken from the publication by C.W. Fronke: *Defrost Your Frozen Assets* (Waco: Word, Inc., 1969).

[2]Mark Gibbs and Ralph Morton, *God's Frozen People* (Philadelphia: The Westminster Press, 1965), p. 6.

[3]From a sermon delivered by Dr. Jitsuo Morikawa, Riverside Church, May 15, 1977.

Doctor Cain H. Felder

D r. Cain Felder is professor of New Testament Studies at Howard University Divinity School. He is editor of the *Journal of Religious Thought*, Howard University Divinity School and Howard University Press. He has just completed his book entitled *Troubling Biblical Waters: Race, Class, Family*, to be published in the fall.

His community-related activities include: community outreach consultant, St. Mark's United Methodist Church, Baltimore, Md. (1973-1974); delegate to Northeast Jurisdictional Conference, the United Methodist Church and alternate delegate to General Conference from Southern New England Annual Conference, UMC (1972); chairman, Union Theological Seminary's Black Economic and Development Committee (1969-1970).

The Cost of Freedom
In Urban Churches

by Cain H. Felder

When the Israelites saw the king and his army marching against them, they were terrified and cried out to the LORD for help. They said to Moses, "Weren't there any graves in Egypt? Did you have to bring us out here in the desert to die? Look what you have done by bringing us out of Egypt! Didn't we tell you before we left this would happen? We told you to leave us alone and let us go on being slaves of the Egyptians. It would be better to be slaves there than to die here in the desert." (Exodus 14:10-12, TEV)

As for you, my brothers, you were called to be free. But do not let this freedom become an excuse for letting your physical desires control you. Instead let love make you serve one another. For the whole Law is summed up in one commandment: "Love your neighbor as you love yourself." ... What I say is this: let the Spirit direct your lives, and you will not satisfy the desires of the human nature. . . . The Spirit produces love, joy, peace, patience, kindness, goodness, faithfulness, humility, and self-control. There is no law against such as these. (Galatians 5:13-14, 16, 22-23, TEV)

We began in our reflections this morning with a dimension of two biblical ideals, namely justice and peace. We suggested that those ideals are certainly important and discerning that might be the basis of a constructive agenda for churches to become involved in a new way in their communities. We suggested, of course, that the context for this involvement, like never before, must be our urban centers. The city beckons and calls us to practice in a new way the agenda of justice as it leads to the shalom of God—the peace of God.

This evening we lift up yet another of these biblical ideas—justice, peace, and now freedom. We need to speak of freedom because the Bible is very much concerned with political and religious freedom. I submit that it is the proper exercise of freedom that helps us to reach out in a new way to the neighbor who is the subject of the royal law of God (James 2:8). Paul, no less than Jesus, reminds us that the whole law is fulfilled in this one precept: "thou shalt love thy neighbor as thyself" (Galatians 5:14). We who stand behind all sorts of walls (which we construct) fail so very often to break down those walls of alienation and hostility and reach out in freedom to our neighbor.

Freedom: Galatians 5:1 tells us that we are called to freedom. Paul, echoing the words of Moses in Exodus 14, reshapes Moses' ancient injunction, showing the adaptability of God's word for every crisis. In the Galatian situation, Paul says: "For freedom, Christ has set us free" (5:1). That's half of the good news; that's the indicative of salvation! The other half is found in Galatians 5:25, "if we live in the Spirit [of freedom], let us *walk* in this Spirit." The supposition is that just as God's grace in the Christ event enables us to live a new life of freedom, we are under a divine mandate to move from the indicative to the imperative of salvation.

The imperative of salvation in Galatians 5:1 is "stand fast in faith." This is what Moses says to the "doubting Thomases" and those persons whose faith is so vitiated the minute there is a bit of struggle, the minute there is a bit of threat, surfacing again now in the hordes or minions of Pharaoh's army. Oh, yes, it's a very human situation, isn't it my friends? Much of our own experience enables us to understand that experience of the Hebrew children. They were like you and me in many respects. They mouth all sorts of faith in God, particularly when they are the beneficiaries of the great miracles as displayed through stages of Moses' prophetic ministry before Pharaoh. The plagues came and were visited upon the Egyptians as a symbol of their need to let the people go, to let them be free, to let them out of the ghettos of Goshen and the cruel cities of Egypt, to let them move forward to the new vision of their future. The Lord had indeed heard the cries of the people! The plagues dramatized the need for Pharaoh to understand the importance of those cries. The plagues are the miracles of God shown to Pharaoh. And as those miracles unfold the Hebrew people are happy. They are joyous, feeling confirmed by the dramatic power of God. As they said, "Yahweh is great!"

And so they walked out of Goshen. They walked out of Egypt with "the taunting high hand" of arrogance. You can imagine them looking back at Pharaoh and the Egyptians as they clean out the granaries and then take all the gold they can find. But as they move toward the Red Sea they find that a new measure of faith is required. A new level of reflection is demanded, reflection on the meaning of the very freedom that they had earlier claimed with such arrogance as they bolted from Goshen and Egypt. Now, they turned around and saw that Pharaoh had not yet given up! He was going to make one last effort, as his heart was hardened, to destroy the children of God as they marched toward the sea. As they saw Pharaoh's chariots coming . . . you know the story. If you haven't read it in the Bible, you certainly remember it from Cecil B. DeMille's movie *The Ten Commandments.* In that film Pharaoh is shown with all the assurance that he will be able to wipe out God's people who are trapped with their backs against the sea.

In their predicament, the people interrogate Moses anew. No longer are they willing to follow him. Suddenly the people raise those pathetic and ridiculous, rhetorical questions which I paraphrase: "Moses, Moses, have you brought us out in the wilderness to die? It would be better for us to have stayed in Egypt and served the slave masters and task masters than to have to discover the responsibility of our freedom out here. What have you done to us, Moses?" Now remember, these are the very people who only a few days earlier had praised Moses for his brilliance and who had professed all measure of faith in God, the Almighty.

But in a minute of difficulty, in a minute of threatening obstacles, their faith dissipates like smoke. But Moses, blessed prophet of God that he is, turns around and simply says to the people, "stand firm and see the salvation of your God" (Exodus 14:13). I can imagine what Moses may have wanted to say if he had been a less righteous person!

As for Moses in Exodus 14, so for Paul in the closing segment of the freedom chapters of Galatians. God's Apostle deals forthrightly with the backsliding tendencies of the members of this church who were not able to nourish and take forward the initial promptings of the gospel message. No sooner had Paul left town than did they succumb to the interlopers and the opponents of Paul who wanted to undermine his ministry among them. "When the cat's away, the mice will play!" The Galatian church quickly showed that they were not so comfortable with Paul's message of freedom after all. Like the Hebrew children, the Galatians wanted to fall back into slave covenants of sorts. "Let us abandon this vision of freedom with its responsibility, and have the comfort and security of being enslaved by one thing or another."

Like Moses, the apostle Paul turns and says to them, "Stand fast for freedom! Christ has set you free!" Let me paraphrase further: "Don't you know that you must stand fast against all principalities and powers, against all interlopers, against all narrow-minded, back-biting gossips and anyone else who'll do the work of the Devil? Stand fast and you will then be able to move in the Spirit with your head up, demonstrating in your life the fruits of the Spirit."

Paul's exhortation has direct application for us here in America who tend to give "lip service" to the word "freedom." Freedom is one of those abstract terms that almost never is defined with precision. In the United States of America, we claim a heritage of freedom. We say that we are the capital of the free world, whatever that means. We say, "the land of the free." Even the Declaration of Independence proclaims liberty or freedom as one of the inalienable rights of human beings. And yet, the men who wrote that document scarcely believed that women, Native Americans or blacks were equal to them or even human. Two hundred years ago, a black basically was regarded as three-fifths of a person, mere property. Furthermore, nearly a century after the Declaration of Independence, there still was need for the Emancipation Proclamation which formally abolished, throughout the nation, the institution of slavery.

In fact, throughout our national history we do not so much encounter a pure form of freedom so much as degrees of freedom, with too much rhetoric about freedom. The fact of the matter is that most people do not wish to be free. Most people tend to resist the responsibility of freedom. We in this country, for all our rhetoric about freedom, have ways of resisting the full responsibility of what it means to be a beacon of freedom in a world of hurt, in a world of despair, in a world of alienation. We lack the courage, particularly when it comes to the dollar, to be free. If it doesn't contribute to our profits, if it doesn't contribute to our selfish aggrandizement and our sense of materialism and self-interest, we don't really care about freedom. How else can we explain our policies in Latin America and our policies in South Africa, as well as other places where obviously there is no freedom? There are apparently other, higher authorities than freedom. Whatever do we mean by calling ourselves the capital of the free world? I do not understand our talk about freedom when we are standing against true democratic yearnings all over the world.

We need a little good news in America today, friends. I'll tell you friends, we could use a little good news in reflecting about the mandate for churches to be involved in their communities. Churches seeking to serve should be serving in the higher key of freedom. For freedom Christ has set us free.

Being a Christian is not merely practicing a knee-jerk exercise of empty rhetoric. This is one of the problems I have with some people in fundamentalist or charismatic movements. They think that all one has to do is to take literally and without references to the larger literary context John 3:16 and Romans 10:9. They then understand salvation as nothing more than mere confessing and believing in Jesus as a guarantee to be saved! But those passages have to be looked at in the original context so that the message of salvation can relate to a mundane moral responsibility. Actually, these texts point us to a whole life of responsible engagement in light of producing the fruits of the Spirit. We must seek both the indicative and imperative of salvation! Stand fast. Christ gives us the possibilities of a new life in the Spirit, but we must walk in the Spirit (Galatians 5:25). Show the fruits of the Spirit and so demonstrate the power of the righteousness of God.

Jacques Ellul makes the important observation that freedom is not an inherited need, since most people seem to prefer security, conformity, adaptation or economy of effort. That is, most people are basically too selfish or lazy to be truly free. They want to take shortcuts. We see it in our schools all the time. My daughter sometimes talks about how to do her school work as a shortcut so she can watch more television. Too often, irrespective of the quality, we are concerned about the economy of effort.

Erich Fromm puts the matter even more forcefully when he notes that human beings have a tendency to submit uncritically to external, often anonymous power. By so doing we lose power and lose true freedom. We lose morality, reverting to prejudice, superstition and fear. You see, friends, when we back away from the freedom to which God in Jesus Christ points us, we lapse into the worst kind of irresponsibility and we fail to understand the vision of God for us. We are supposed to be agents of the righteousness of God, which like never before urban communities need to feel and to see in tangible human activity and in the work of the church. Even though Fromm writes about the plight of modern persons, one can apply his description of the human dilemma to persons within the Galatian church of antiquity. Paul issues again the divine call to freedom, but the Galatians are obviously fearful of the personal and social responsibilities that come with such freedom.

Sometimes I refer to this problem as it happens in Jesus' ministry. Recall those people who have so many problems to bring to Jesus. Theirs is the syndrome of the "gimmes." They want something for nothing. "Gimme this. Gimme that." Don't you know even in our prayer life we have this syndrome of "gimmes"? "Lord, can you give me this, can you give me that?" And seldom do we ask the Lord, "How might you use me in a new way in service to my neighbor? How might you teach me what it means to be a free person?" Those are not oftentimes our prayer, but should be, my friends.

Consider again the freedom chapters of Galatians. Chapters 3 through 5 of Galatians represent the "freedom chapters" just as chapters 5 through 8 of Romans constitute the freedom chapters of that more reflective piece. In a sense, these freedom chapters are foundational for Paul's message, because he wants to show that freedom is principally about making choices. Through the Christ event (the death and resurrection of Jesus), we are freed up from all kinds of slave covenants. We are freed from the law.

But too often we try to reckon our merit to guarantee salvation. Many of us in the churches are like this, always trying to prove that we are saved, instead of resonating and rolling with what it means to be saved, letting it show forth—letting your light shine. We worry too much about who is benefitting from the light. Let it shine and let persons benefit who are your neighbors. What we need is to be free *from* our self-preoccupations and all the related negatives in our lives.

But it's not enough to be free *from* something, we must also determine what we are free *for.* What are our urban churches free *for* in our communities? What is the constructive agenda that is supposed to be free to escape? I think that Paul makes it very clear in Galatians 5 that we are to produce new life in the Spirit. We should be freed up to recognize that freedom is ultimately going to *cost* something. We have to be prepared to pay freedom's true price. Yes, it may cost us in terms of our time. It may cost us in terms of our egos. It may cost us in terms of the pew we like to sit in or the committee chair we have. It may cost us a sense of our schedules and our own privately organized and orchestrated priorities. It's going to cost you something! It may cost you some funds. It may cost another late night when you have to plan something for people you believe don't even appreciate what you are doing. It's going to cost you something.

But you have been freed in the Spirit to make these responsible choices—to have the ability to respond. That is why I like to spell "responsibility" with a hyphen: response-ability. Dr. Luther E. Smith suggests such a spelling in *God in Human Freedom,* the Festschrift or dedication volume that Henry Young edited honoring Dr. Howard Thurman. Response-ability, because freedom makes a new kind of partnership in assessing before God your ability to be responsible, to be involved in urban areas. What is your ability to be responsive; to respond to the needs, to the brokenness all around? Yes, freedom *costs.* The danger is that we have too many abuses of freedom in our cities. In contradistinction to those abuses of freedom, we have the biblical call to a responsible sense of freedom that produces the fruits of the Spirit.

You may well ask, "What did freedom mean to that black American slave woman who on April 9, 1865, witnessed the Confederate flag suddenly being lowered in the sign of surrender in Richmond, Virginia?" The answer is in Vincent Harding's very helpful and carefully documented book, *There Is a River; The Black Struggle for Freedom in America.* He presents her sheer ecstasy in a few pages. You can hear her now:

> Run to the kitchen and shout in the window, "Mammy, you don't have to cook no more, you is free, you is free, don't you know?" Run to the henhouse and shout to the rooster, "Rooster, don't crow no more, you is free too." Go to the pigpen and tell the old pig, "You is free; you don't have to grunt no more . . . no more, no more . . . You is free." Praising Father God, kissing Mother Earth, running and loving with all their creatures, you is free, you is free."

In a certain sense that black woman felt in an essentially important way what it means to be on the threshold of a bold new mode of access to freedom!

But freedom *costs* if we take it seriously. We in the church need to know that freedom has its price. Freedom certainly costs, because freedom, as Paul tells us, is really an inalienable right. Nevertheless, it is irrevocable, Paul says with reference to the divine call in Romans 12. When you responded at your baptism, when you responded in your formal call to the ministry, when you responded by joining a church, you responded to the call to be something new as part of the new creation to be free, but throughout you have been fighting on behalf of the irrevocable nature of the call to freedom. You can try to deny it. I certainly, in my life, have tried to deny my call, lapsing back from time to time. But you know, God has a way of just presenting the divine reality in many different symbolic guises and on different occasions. Just when you think you are running away and hiding under a big enough bush or behind a tall enough tree, God will catch you and remind you that the call is irrevocable. God wants you and the people to be free. God wants you to know that sense of freedom, my friends.

Oh, the invitation that we find in Paul's words reiterated in 2 Corinthians 3:17 is a marvelous thing: "Where the Spirit of the Lord is, there is freedom." There is freedom as we open ourselves to God's Spirit in our midst and open ourselves to what Howard Thurman called the inner religious experience of God. We can become transformed to be truly a free people who know the things that make for peace and justice and neighborly concern through our lives. Paul sums up the whole law by referring to the moral substance of the Christ event. He cites in Galatians 5:14 the Law which in James 2:8 becomes the "Royal Law" to love your neighbor. The Spirit produces this in human life, in your communities, if you will let it. The results are such fruit of the Spirit as love, joy, peace, patience, kindness, generosity, fidelity, tolerance and self-control. And we don't even have to speak about the Law; the grace of God in the Christ event has removed Law as the motive.

Even if a person should be detected in some sin, my brother, the spiritual ones among you should quietly set him back on the right path. Don't just go out and condemn the teenage parents who made those terrible mistakes, or the young people in our communities who are using drugs, or the people in our households who have problems with gambling or alcohol, whose lives are dysfunctional because of their bad choices. Don't just put them down and throw them out and speak mean to them. But somehow pray for the strength to be able to say the healing word and remind them that they, too, despite the difficulties, can be restored in a new sense of power that will conform to the vision that God has for them. Oh, my friends, don't you know when Paul says, "carry one another's burdens and so live out the law of Christ," it's nothing but the perfect and sublime law of freedom? "For freedom has set you free. Stand fast, therefore, in that freedom and do not submit again to the yoke of slavery." Amen.

[1]Vincent Harding, *There Is a River: The Black Struggle for Freedom in America* (New York: Random House Inc., 1983).

The Reverend
Marsha Brown Woodard

Rev. Marsha Brown Woodard is a consultant to religious and social service organizations and associate pastor of the Saints Memorial Baptist Church in Bryn Mawr, Pennsylvania. She has previously served on the staffs of the Board of Educational Ministries and the Antioch Baptist Church in St. Louis, Mo. Marsha is a graduate of Ottawa University in Ottawa, Kansas, and Eden Theological Seminary, Webster Groves, Mo. She has written articles for a variety of publications, and is editor of *Making Sense of Your Faith.* She currently resides in King of Prussia, Pa.

"Dream Keepers"

by Rev. Marsha B. Woodard

Thus says God, the LORD, who created the heavens and stretched them out, who spread forth the earth and what comes from it, who gives breath to the people upon it–and spirit to those who walk in it; "I am the LORD, I have called you in righteousness, I have taken you by the hand and kept you; I have given you as a covenant to the people, a light to the nations, to open the eyes that are blind, to bring out the prisoners from the dungeon, from the prison those who sit in darkness. I am the LORD, that is my name: my glory I give to no other, nor my praise to graven images. Behold, the former things have come to pass, and new things I now declare: before they spring forth I tell you of them." (Isaiah 42:5-9)

What happens to a dream deferred?
Does it dry up
    like a raisin in the sun?
Or fester like a sore
    —and then run?
Does it stink
    like rotten meat?
Or crust and sugar over
    like a syrupy sweet?
Maybe it just sags like a heavy load
    or does it explode?

Langston Hughes[1]

What happens to a dream deferred? What happens when God's dream seems to be deferred? What happens to God's dream of a world where people live in harmony—a world where the hungry are fed, where the stranger is welcomed, a world where instruments of war become instruments of peace? What happens to God's dream of a world, where justice and righteousness prevail, where people work with God to show other people new ways of living, where the last become first, where little becomes much?

What happens when those entrusted with the dream have become indifferent to the dream, when those entrusted with the dream have become blind to the possibilities of its fulfillment, when those called to be dream keepers are in fact dream deferrers?

What happens to a dream deferred? As I began to think about what it means to care, I discovered I couldn't think about care without thinking about the dream. It seems to me that God's dream and care must be kept in tension.

For what does care really mean? Do we care, as the people of God, the same as others? Does it make a difference if we feel a "calling" to care? Is care just giving a smile or a hug? Is caring just providing food or shelter? What do we mean when we say "God's people," not just anybody but the people of God, are "called" to care?

I'm convinced that the caring we do must be different—it must be rooted in God's dream. The Bible attests to this dream (of God's) in both the Old and New Testaments. Our Scripture from Isaiah speaks of that dream of God: who created this world and to make it complete created humankind to be in covenant with God, a people to be a light to other nations, a people living in new ways so that others might learn to live in new ways. We learn of this dream over and over again, and it continues in the New Testament as God gives his only begotten Son, Jesus, that through Jesus the world might be reconciled with God and humankind might understand in new ways what it means to be the people of God.

This dream of God includes the rights of the poor being

upheld. This dream has an inclusive community, a community where diversity is affirmed—where each gift is recognized because each gift is needed. This dream of God includes a world ordered by different priorities; it's this dream that has been entrusted to us.

It sounds so simple that our first thought is *of course we are keepers of the dream, of course we wouldn't do anything to defer the dream; of course, we care like God cares*—but do we? Do we really love God with all our heart, mind and soul? Do we really seek first God's kingdom and God's righteousness? Or have we at times become indifferent to the dream? Do we really keep the dream or have we sometimes become guilty of claiming other dreams and trying to play them off as God's dream? Have we sometimes become like a group of Christians I heard about who were so caught up in their own thing that they couldn't be involved in God's thing? I'm sure this wouldn't happen to any churches here, but this group received a memo from Jesus that went a little like this:

Dear Christians:

I've been authorized by God to send you this memorandum. You are to go to all people everywhere and call them to be my disciples. You are to baptize them and teach them the meaning of the commandments which I have given you. I'll never forsake you, because I love you so much. Please don't forget about me and our work together.

With all my love,
Jesus Christ

Of course, such a memo called for a response, and they did in fact respond:

Dear Jesus,

We acknowledge receipt of your memo. Your proposal is both interesting and challenging. However, due to a shortage in personnel, as well as several financial and personal obligations, we do not feel that we can give proper emphasis to your challenge at this time.

A committee (task force) has been appointed to study your plan and its feasibility and should have a response to bring before our congregation in the near future. You may rest assured that we will give it our very careful consideration and that all of our boards (and committees) will think about it for future action. We appreciate your offer to serve as our resource consultant should we care to undertake this project sometime in the future.

Cordially,
The Christians (Adapted)

It sounds a little unbelievable—nothing we would ever do, for we wouldn't write such a response—but have we not in other ways sometimes given a similar response? Have we not found ourselves sometimes saying, "That sounds like a good way to live but not right now"? Have we not said, "Sure, God, we could have other priorities but not this year"? "Yes, God, I guess we could tackle that project but a bigger church could do it more easily"? No, we haven't written a response, but our actions have sometimes said, "God, we'll put you on hold for just a little while."

To be keepers of the dream means we must speak a new word—we must say that peace cannot be found in nuclear weapons, that justice is not taking over other countries just because we're bigger. To be keepers of the dream is to stand and say there are enough funds to provide homes, education, food, basic needs for all. We have simply chosen to use them for other things. To be keepers of the dream is to say Jesus is Lord and God is God and our lives are rooted in their dream.

The world needs us to be dream keepers. The world needs us because we've been sent for this age. We have been entrusted with the dream. We can be dream keepers. We can be the people God needs, for God throughout the ages has used ordinary people to be keepers of the dream. It's not easy but we can do it. For I have it on good authority that God will use folks like me and you.

God called Abraham and Sarah when they were old and told them to leave their homeland and go to a new land. From them we learn that we, too, can trust God to show us new lands, new opportunities.

I read about two midwives, Shiphrah and Puah, who stood up against the Pharaoh, and from them we learn that we can stand against the powers and principalities of our age.

And there was Jethro, Moses' father-in-law, who helped Moses understand a new way of organization, a model of shared leadership which helps us understand that we can develop new structures, new systems of leadership for our day.

Though in exile, Mordecai helped Esther to remember her roots so she could be all that God would have her be. We need to help each other remember our roots, to remember to whom we belong that we might be all that God would have us be.

You remember that poor widow who put her all in the offering to show us that we can give our all, not just our extra.

Even Zacchaeus, when salvation came, radically changed his priorities, which helps us remember that we, too, can change priorities.

Yes, we can be dream keepers, for there have been persons keeping the dream throughout history—folks like:

Kathy Ferguson, who started Sunday schools;
Lott Carey, Ann and Adoniram Judson, and Lulu Fleming, who were missionaries;
Helen Barrett Montgomery, who translated the New Testament;
Sojourner Truth, Frederick Douglass, and Harriet Tubman, who spoke out for the rights of blacks;
Ida Wells Barnett, who worked for justice for all people.

God will use us to continue the dream in the future. God needs dream keepers like you and me who are willing to give their all no matter how small it might seem; folks like you and me who believe that with God all things are possible; folks like you and me who believe that we can do all things through Christ who strengthens us; folks like you and me who lose our lives and then find life.

We can care. We can be dream keepers. We can work to

make God's dream our dream and that dream a reality on this
earth.

[1]Langston Hughes, "Dream Deferred" from "Harlem" segment of "Montage of a
Dream Deferred" in *Selected Poems* (New York: Alfred A. Knopf Inc., 1974), p. 26.
Used by permission.

Epilogue

A Sense of Urgency

by Miles Jerome Jones

For this Vision of Hope through Church-Based Community Development to become reality, each American Baptist congregation will need to develop a sense of urgency on the basis of congregational self-understanding and identification of mission.

To the extent a congregation interprets its role in the light of the call of God, its vision will include this community-oriented opportunity with the following elements:

EMPOWERMENT OF PERSONS will be a major goal of all congregational activities. This goal cuts across economic or social divisions. It is as valuable for the affluent as for the impoverished. All sectors of our society must see themselves with power to effect changes which money cannot provide. Individuals will make a difference through the "power of our being." The power of our being concerned, being related, being willing to risk and being rewarded in other than monetary terms are the things which empower our ability to get things done on behalf of persons.

NEW CONGREGATIONAL METHODOLOGIES will be evident as one part of the congregation's response to community development concerns. For example, with a sense of urgent necessity churches must recapture the movement model of the early church without abandoning the advantages of structures and mechanisms which help to produce efficient utilization of resources. The key will be flexibility within organizational parameters. As organizational structures are flexible, the congregation will be able to move in response to community needs.

The sense of urgency will be as practical as the current social needs of a community, many of which are evident in the daily newspaper. All the ills that beset communities are to be addressed wholistically by congregations. For example, just as the church should demand the arrest of drug dealers in the neighborhood, it might also provide a prison ministry for the same persons when they are arrested and convicted. If need be, the congregation could provide assistance for families who may be disadvantaged as a result of the arrest the church has encouraged. In short, each congregation must be organized for the task of ministering the wide range of needs as reflected in the community in which the church is located.

Church-Based Community Development is the response of each congregation to its own community. The Board of National Ministries stands ready to provide resources, but each American Baptist congregation must respond to the urgent call of God to a ministry providing Visions of Hope to persons in need.